Being Your

D0924951

We End

This thoughtful book asks young people to consider the crucial question: "Who do you want to be?" rather than "What do you want to be?" One's personal choices and character are the greatest determinants of an individual's success and happiness in life. Each chapter focuses on a key concept, using stories, affirmations, and exercises to deeply engage the reader. It is perfectly formated not only for the individual reader, but also for weekly discussion groups such as scouts, religious groups, and counseling groups. We highly recommend this inspiring book!

Bernard B. Wolfberg, MD, Psychiatrist
Laura L. Robinson, PhD, Psychologist

Mahatma Gandhi said that you must be the change you wish to see in the world. As the young adults of today take on the formidable task of trying to create a future that is dynamic, innovative and progressive but also peaceful, kind and sane they need to begin by living those attributes themselves. Kathy Poodiack's "Being Your Best Self" is the quintessential guidebook for living a life that is not only deeply happy, but profoundly self-aware. An easy read with awe-inspiring stories to illustrate every concept, it should be required reading for any young adult who wants to live consciously and be a true contribution to the world. If "Being Your Best Self" were required reading, this world would be a completely different place to live.

Debra Poneman, best-selling author and founder of
Yes to Success Seminars, Inc.

This book is truly amazing! It's very easy to read and I believe that doing the exercises in each chapter will add to its impact. Both my high school and college students could benefit greatly from it.

Yana Teplitsky,
School Counselor, Teacher, and Mother

Ms. Poodiack has created an optimistic and encouraging book that will help people looking to lead a fuller life through "conscious living". Acceptance of self and others is an old message that Ms. Poodiack reminds us of and gives some step-by-step guidance on helping us along that path.

Richard E. Kast, MD, Psychiatrist

This is a very well put together self-help book! I have been through so many obstacles in my life, never understanding my purpose or place in the world. The day I decided it was time for me to put alcohol away for good was the day my entire life changed, but it wasn't that decision alone that proceeded to help me live a better life. It was the extensive amount of reading of self-help books that assisted my transformation in a major way. I reverse engineered, then recreated myself and the results were like nothing I had ever imagined. I now have this book to add to my collection. I appreciate the reference of stories combined with exercises that remind me that I need to keep self aware, appreciate myself and understand the value that I contribute to the world. I absolutely love the consistency of empowerment that creates a sense of inspiration and motivation. Kathy talks about influence. When I finally realized who I was and what my purpose was in life it was transformational. We are all connected, like it says in the book, and we can choose the attitude in which we want to influence people in this world. I love that this book is written for young people who may need some guidance in living a more fulfilling life. Thank you, Kathy for a great read!

Matthew Cohen, Entrepreneur

This is a book of life skills for anyone and everyone, no matter your age, gender or religion. "Being Your Best Self" reads like your best, smartest, sweetest friend sharing wisdom in a warm and motivating conversation.

Toba Frankel, PhD
Family Therapist, Learning Disabilities Specialist

Kathy Poodiack has managed to explain "Being Your Best Self" in an easily understandable way. It is a topic that is very near to the hearts of many young adults.

Sarah Frohlinger, High School Sophomore

Being Your Best Self

A Young Adult's Guide to Conscious Living

Kathy Poodiack, PA-C

Mazo Publishers

Being Your Best Self

ISBN: 978-1-94612412-8

Contact the author by email
guidetoconsciousliving@gmail.com

Be a Facebook Friend
www.facebook.com/
guidetoconsciousliving/

Published by

Mazo Publishers
P.O. Box 10474
Jacksonville, FL 32247 USA

www.mazopublishers.com
mazopublishers@gmail.com

~ To my husband, Jim ~

*Thank you for your unwavering support
throughout my many journeys of self-discovery
and for helping me become my best self.*

The Author

Kathy Poodiack is a certified oncology Physician Assistant (PA-C), researcher, wife, mother and grandmother. As a result of caring for terminally ill people for the past 35 years, Kathy has developed a passion for life, which she shares with everyone she meets.

Kathy is especially interested in the mental health of young adults, believing that this generation holds the keys to the future of our planet. Through "Being Your Best Self" Kathy encourages her readers to appreciate life's gifts now rather than waiting for a crisis to "turn yourself around." She also teaches about self-esteem and tolerance, which many young adults struggle with daily.

Kathy believes that every person has the capacity to make a difference in their lifetime and this book is one of her contributions.

Contents

INTRODUCTION

*The only person you are destined to become
is the person you decide to be.*
~ Ralph Waldo Emerson

Don't you wish you had a dollar for every time someone asked you ... "What do you want to be when you grow up"? And don't you wish you had another dollar for every time you gave some random answer just so they would stop asking?

Now, just think how broke you would be if you had a dollar for every time someone asked you ... "Who do you want to be when you grow up"?

When was the last time someone asked you ... "What kind of person do you want to be?" "What kind of life do you want to live?" "What kind of relationships do you want to have?" "How do you want people to treat you?"

And if someone did ask, do you know how you would answer?

Just as you need to plan a course of action to attain any goal, **you also need a plan for becoming the kind of person you want to be.**

At the time when I was growing up, young adults didn't have to think too much about the kind of person they wanted to be because they had people around them who served as role models, who took them under their wing, mentored them and gave good advice.

Usually one parent stayed at home so they had much more time to spend with their kids and could talk with them more often. They had time to share their experiences, teach life lessons and give encouragement.

Kids looked up to sports figures because they represented perseverance and strength. Religious leaders were highly respected and revered. They offered comfort and guidance in times of need. Teachers and coaches were mentors to their students and players and had time to give a little extra when they could see there was someone in need of a little more attention.

My husband coached middle school and high school sports. He was a true mentor to his players and taught them a lot about life through sports. He taught them about respect, cooperation, loyalty and fair play. When one of his players was having a tough time at home, he would stay with us for a while until things improved. We loved helping them and the parents appreciated it as well.

It pains me to say that today, in the 21st century, these role models are the exception rather than the rule. In America, fifty percent of children live in a divorce situation where they only have access to one parent at a time.[1] Due to tough economic times, that parent usually needs to work full-time and may have more than one job just to make ends meet. Often, the most advice they have time to give is "do your homework" and "brush your teeth." You may or may not see your parent before everyone leaves home for the day, and in the evening everyone is busy taking care of their own needs. There's little time for discussing the day, let alone life in general.

Today, when you read or listen to the news reports, its seems like there is another story about a sports figure who's been banned from participating due to doping or cheating or sometimes something even worse.

Many religious figures are far from the pillars of righteousness we once thought they were. Unfortunately, because of their own weaknesses, they are hardly the ones to be offering advice about virtuous living.

When teachers have to deal with large classes of 40 students in a period, they hardly have time to teach, let alone take an interest in each individual student. Coaches are forced to focus on athletic performance and winning rather than what's going on in their players' heads.

---

1   American Psychological Association: http://www.apa.org/topics/divorce/

So where does this leave you? Hopefully, you do have at least one person you can count on as a role model, who can guide you and be there for you.

If you don't, then I want you to know I'm here for you, communicating with you through this book.

This book will be like your personal GPS, to get you on course and keep you there, helping you become your best self. However, if you want to learn from me and my experiences, you need to know that it's not enough for me that you become a decent, caring human being. I also want you to learn how to live what's called **"a conscious life."**

Reach for the stars! Learn to stretch beyond your limits of today and attain all that you desire. When you live **a conscious life,** you can be happy and content and contribute to this planet in the best possible way.

The way most people live nowadays is what's called "unconscious living." Unconscious living is like going through life with blinders on. It's feeling that you don't matter, that you don't deserve to be happy, that you're here to suffer. It's being fearful of the future and regretting the past, and rarely living in the present. It's being suspicious of other people.

Unconscious living is about intimidating other people or tearing them down so you can feel superior. It's living as a follower rather than a leader. It's believing that because of your family situation or your "genes" or some other such nonsense, you'll never have financial security and will work hard your entire life just to scrape by. It's hiding in virtual realities so you don't have to face your day or getting an artificial high from drugs and alcohol because not being high is too painful. It's about waiting until a point of crisis in your life before you decide to make changes.

Believe me, I know this from experience. As a health care provider, a Physician Assistant caring for people with cancer, I have witnessed miraculous transformations in people. It's amazing what changes people can make when faced with their own mortality. **The key is to make the changes before a crisis hits.**

Conscious living means breaking through these limitations. It's about opening your mind to a whole new world of possibilities. It's about believing that you matter, that you have worth and that you deserve the best that life has to offer. It's about realizing that you weren't put on this planet to suffer, but to be happy and productive. It's about realizing that you can have anything and everything you have ever wanted if you just open yourself up to receiving.

Conscious living is about realizing that

everyone on this planet is connected, that we can live together peacefully by tolerating and appreciating our differences and focusing on our similarities. It's about doing what you know is right, about giving love and receiving love. It's about spending time with the people you care about and showing them how much you appreciate them. It's about taking responsibility for your actions, learning from your mistakes and committing to do better. It's about staying present, learning from the past and letting go of regrets. It's about having goals, but not living for the future.

Conscious living is about surrounding yourself with people and things that will contribute to your full potential and help keep your energy high. It's about realizing that unlimited possibilities lie ahead of you and believing that **anything is possible**. It's about letting go of fear and being courageous enough to be creative and curious and willing to learn as much as you can about the world around you. It's about putting things into your body that only contribute to your highest good. It's about finding something, anything to be grateful for.

Conscious living opens you up to happiness, contentment, balance and wholeness.

All that is required of you to live a conscious life is to shift your thinking and let what lies

within you to surface and shine.

Just the mere fact that you're reading this book now means that you're ready to learn how to live a conscious life. You don't have to wait until you're older and hope that you figure it all out then. Most likely, you'll still be lost, and have lived a few more years of unconscious living.

Why do you think there are so many self-help books written for adults? Because no one taught them how to be happy before they reached adulthood. And no one ever asked them when they were younger, "Who do you want to be?" I want to share this life-changing information with you.

As I said, for the past 35 years in my professional career, I have cared for people with cancer. I have witnessed a lot of suffering. I've had patients die in my arms. Life is too short. I don't want you to be the one with regrets, thinking about what you could've or should've done or said, or the person you could've been.

Decide who you want to be and start being that person. This is the ideal time – you're old enough to understand this book and young enough to make lasting changes.

I'm one of those people who, for years, has been reading every self-help book I could get my hands on and attending conferences and workshops. Then, at around age 50, I learned about conscious living and finally, I got it. I learned how to access the treasures that lie within me and I stopped looking for answers outside myself.

Now, I'm the happiest I've ever been. I'm living a life that, to me, is perfect and I have everything I want. And it's not just me. I know many people who have made this shift in awareness and they, too, are the happiest and most content they have ever been.

Let me tell you about my friend Claire. She became pregnant when she was young. She and her boyfriend got married, even though both knew there was no love between them. They had another child and stayed married for 26 years. Their marriage was wrought with tension, anger, and frustration. They each stayed in a different part of the house to avoid the other. The husband numbed himself with alcohol. He eventually found someone else and asked for a divorce.

Claire was devastated. Not because she loved him, but because it was all she knew. She was miserable, but she was comfortable.

Once the divorce was final, she made the decision to start a new life, leave her comfort zone and move forward.

By practicing conscious living, Claire opened herself up to unlimited possibilities and abundance. She decided that she wasn't too old to start over and that she deserved to have a wonderful life with a perfect partner. Within a few months, she connected with a man online, they met and fell madly in love. They're now touring different parts of Europe together. Never in my friend's wildest dreams did she think she would ever be living this kind of life. She now feels loved, fulfilled and excited about each new day.

Another friend of mine had a very rocky relationship with her daughter for many years. It got to a point where the daughter cut off all contact with her. After three years of this, my friend learned about shifting her consciousness and instead of blaming herself and being angry with her daughter, she decided to focus on the love she had for her and every day would send her thoughts of forgiveness and understanding.

In her mind's eye, she would send healing energy to her daughter and visualized them having wonderful conversations. Within a very short time, the daughter called my friend and apologized for not being in contact with her for so long, asked for forgiveness and they renewed their relationship which continues to this day.

But, you don't have to wait until you are middle-aged to have a wonderful life. You can have it NOW!

The material I am sharing with you has been garnered from the leaders in the world of conscious living – their concepts and teachings. My goal is to present this information in a way that you can relate to. There are many books written about each one of these concepts and you can delve deeper at any time. (See the recommended reading list at the end of the book.)

In each chapter of this book, I first introduce a concept, tell a story to illustrate the idea, and then at the end, offer you positive statements to say, and exercises for you to do to help you make the shift in awareness and internalize the idea and the feelings it evokes.

As you read each chapter, stay open and nonjudgmental. Make an intention when starting each one that you will willingly receive the messages and gifts it has to offer and make a commitment to try at least one of the exercises.

Repetition is the key. Your subconscious will take its direction from you and will eventually transform the idea into belief and then into reality.

Trust me. This really does work. You'll see your life change in miraculous ways. You will feel completely different, people will act differently toward you, new opportunities will present themselves and things will appear to you just when you need them to. This is called synchronicity, and it really does happen! You'll handle stressful situations with calm and ease.

Everything will change for the better and you'll see positive changes in the people around you as well.

When you change your energy, it affects the energy of everyone and everything around you. This is one of the greatest gifts you can ever give yourself and others.

I have faith in you. I know you can be your best self, live the life of your dreams, make a positive contribution to society and eventually become a role model for the next generation.

Chapter 1

You Matter

Tell me that I matter and I will prove that you are right.

~ *Unknown author*

On your way to becoming your best self, before you learn anything else, you must first believe that you matter and that you have worth. This is crucial. This is fact. You are here. And if you're here, you matter. You wouldn't be here if you didn't belong here. Despite what anyone may have told you, no one is ever a mistake. The world wouldn't be the same without you in it. If you weren't here, there would be a piece missing from the world. You have a unique energy that no one else on this planet has and it brings the entire energy of the planet to completion. You do make a difference.

I hope you realize this already, but if you don't, you MUST believe this. If you don't, is it because you're afraid to matter? When you believe that you matter, responsibility comes with that realization. People may want your opinion about things, they may expect you to be someone who you don't believe you can be. Don't be afraid. If people ask your opinion, it's because they think it has value. If they expect you to act in a responsible way, it's because they believe that you are capable of that behavior.

One day I was putting a puzzle together with one of my grandchildren. We worked for over an hour and finally got to the last corner of the picture. The last piece of the puzzle was missing from the box. The empty space was directly in the center of the picture. We searched and searched, but couldn't find it anywhere. My grandson looked up at me and said, "Oh well, we ALMOST finished it." I was glad that he could stop the activity and walk away unaffected, but it bothered me to no end. We had worked for so long and all of it was in vain. A puzzle is never "almost" finished. A puzzle is only a puzzle when the picture has been completed, when every single piece is present, linked to its neighbors. That missing piece unwittingly stole the entire essence of the activity.

You are that puzzle piece. You may have brothers and sisters, friends, classmates and teammates whom you think could take your place if you weren't here. But none of them are you. You're unique and there is no one else in the entire world exactly like you, so how could any of them possibly take your place? If you weren't here, your family, class and team would lose their true essence. You are here for a reason. You are here to contribute and to make life a little bit better for everyone you come in contact with.

Fred Rogers of the old children's TV show, Mr. Roger's Neighborhood, summed it up nicely, "If only you could sense how important you are to the lives of those you meet; how important you can be to people you may never even dream of. There is something of yourself that you leave at every meeting with another person."

Lisa

Mrs. Brown liked to shop at the grocery store on Long Avenue. She liked the brands they carried and she liked the wide aisles and the easy to push grocery carts. Most of all, Mrs. Brown liked Lisa, one of the young workers at the meat counter.

Lisa was lucky enough to be hired at the store over summer vacation and even though she was young she loved to cook and this helped get her the job. Whenever Mrs. Brown had a question about something, she always asked for Lisa, because she usually had the answer or she would make the effort to quickly find out from someone who did.

One day, Mrs. Brown went into the store to buy a few things for dinner. She went to the meat counter and wanted some ideas on how best to prepare it. She looked for Lisa, but didn't see her. She asked Laurie, one of the other staff members and was told that Lisa was off for a few days. Mrs. Brown was disappointed, but went ahead and asked Laurie her question. Laurie didn't know the answer, so she left the counter to ask some of the other store workers, but became distracted and it took quite a while until she returned to the meat counter with an answer for Mrs. Brown. Mrs. Brown bought the meat and headed home, somewhat annoyed. She went to the bus stop, but because she had been in the store for so long, she missed the bus and had to wait a long time for the next one. While she waited, it began to rain. She was soaked and a few days later came down with a cold. Then, because Mrs. Brown was ill, she couldn't meet her friend, Doris, for lunch. Doris was an elderly woman who lived alone and looked forward to her weekly lunch with Mrs. Brown. When Mrs. Brown had to cancel their lunch date, Doris was extremely disappointed and became depressed knowing that she would have to wait another whole week for another lunch date.

Mrs. Brown recovered, and a few weeks later, she returned to the store. She stopped by the meat counter and there was Lisa standing behind the counter, greeting Mrs. Brown with a big smile. Mrs. Brown was so happy to see her and told her about her day a few weeks back. She said to Lisa, "you have no idea how your absence affected not only my whole day, but my entire week and my friend's as well." Lisa was so surprised. She never would have thought her presence or absence at work would make such a difference to other people. She realized then that she really did matter.

Affirmations

Affirmations are positive statements that, when said or thought repeatedly, help your subconscious mind accept a new way of thinking. Your new, positive thoughts replace the old, negative ones. This new way of thinking then helps to create a new reality for yourself.

To get the most out of the affirmations in this book, it's best to say them when in a relaxed state. This will help your subconscious mind incorporate them easier and more quickly. To get relaxed, sit in a comfortable chair or lie down on your back. Take a few deep breaths, slowly inhaling and exhaling. When you inhale, try to expand your belly rather than your chest and when you exhale, bring your belly in toward your spine. This is called yogic breathing and is more effective for relaxation than your normal way of breathing.

Starting with your toes and gradually working your way up your body to your head, focus on relaxing each part – your toes, feet, calves, thighs, buttocks, back, abdomen, chest, hands, forearms, shoulders, and face. When you are completely relaxed, repeat the following sentences a few times each or if you prefer, just start with one and you can add the others when it feels right. If there are sentences that make you feel uncomfortable, don't say them. Eventually you may change your mind.

Some people say that affirmations don't work because if you don't believe in what's being said, you feel like you're lying to yourself. It may seem like this at first, but the more you practice it, the easier it becomes and the more you start believing what you're telling yourself. At a certain point, it will feel completely natural and will make perfect sense to you. Eventually it will feel right and truthful. Also, try to repeat them to yourself as many times a day as you can. The best time is right before you fall asleep at night and when you first wake up in the morning before you get out of bed. Of course, in the morning you'll probably just want to say the sentences without the relaxation process so you don't fall back asleep!

If you prefer, you can write the sentences several times each instead of saying them. Don't use a computer. Write them with paper and pen.

This helps your subconscious accept the idea easier. And, best is to do both – say and write them, if you can. What you're doing is training your subconscious mind. It doesn't know the difference between reality and fantasy so it will take direction from your conscious mind and will believe anything you tell it if practiced enough. Just think about all the negative things people have told you in the past and how you came to believe them about yourself. Now is the time to replace those destructive ideas with constructive ones. I'll tell you more about this later.

To Say:
◊   I matter.
◊   I belong here.
◊   I make a difference.
◊   The world wouldn't be the same without me in it.

To Do:
Exercise 1: Make a list of ...
◊   Your strengths
◊   Your accomplishments
◊   Everything you like about yourself.

Don't be modest, shy or negative. No one but you needs to see this. I want you to appreciate YOU and realize all that you have to offer. If your list isn't that long, perhaps by the time you finish reading this book, it will be much longer. You can always add to it as you learn and grow.

Exercise 2:
◊ Think about something you do that involves or affects other people in your life. For example chores, sports, charity work, a club at school, etc.
◊ Now think about how different the energy surrounding that activity would be if you weren't involved in it.
◊ How would your absence affect the outcome of the activity?
◊ How would your absence affect the other people involved?
◊ How would it be different today? tomorrow? a month or a year from now?

You may want to start a journal to accompany this book and write down your answers to these questions and the others that follow in the next chapters plus any other thoughts you may have. Journaling is very therapeutic and can really help you release some emotional energy and work things out in your mind.

Chapter 2

We're All Connected

All things are bound together. All things connect.

~ *Chief Seattle, Suquamish Tribe chief*

Now that you know you matter and that you belong here, the next step is to realize how you fit into the big picture, how your puzzle piece connects with all the others to make one complete beautiful creation.

In her book, "The Field", Lynne McTaggart states:

◊ "All matter exists in a vast quantum web of connection and that an information transfer is constantly going on between living things and their environment."

◊ "At our most elemental, we are not a chemical reaction, but an energetic charge. Human beings and all living things are a coalescence of energy in a field of energy connected to every other thing in the world."

◊ "All matter in the universe is interconnected by waves, which are spread out through

time and space and can carry on to infinity,
tying one part of the universe to every
other part."

This is one of the most exciting discoveries of
modern day physics – that everything is made of
energy, and that includes you. Our bodies consist
of energy that extends beyond our physical selves
and have influence on and intersect with the
energy fields of everyone and everything else
on the planet. It's even been proven that energy
fields separated by very long distances have an
impact on each other.

Behaviorist William Braud found that "people
were more likely to succeed if, instead of believing
in a distinction between themselves and the
world, and seeing individual people and things as
isolated and divisible, they viewed everything as a
connected continuum of interrelations – and also
if they understood that there were other ways to
communicate than through the usual channels."

He goes on to say "our natural state of being
is a relationship – a tango – a constant state of
one influencing the other. Just as the subatomic
particles that compose us cannot be separated
from the space and particles surrounding them,
so living beings cannot be isolated from each
other."

So, because we're all connected because we
share our energies, we all have the ability to

influence each other. The question is, how will YOU choose to influence others and how will you choose to be influenced by those around you?

Your goal should be to keep your energy vibrating at a high level as much as you can. This high energy will be felt knowingly or unknowingly by others and will have a direct impact on how people interact with you. When your energy is high you'll find that people will be nicer and more respectful toward you and will want to be around you and they may not even know why.

Here are some ways you can raise your energy:
◊ Think positively and be optimistic.
◊ Listen to music that makes you happy.
◊ Eat healthy food.
◊ Wear clothes that make you feel good.
◊ Arrange your bedroom so you feel comforted when you enter it.
◊ Watch TV shows and movies that leave you with a good feeling.
◊ Perform acts of kindness.
◊ Volunteer
◊ Meditate
◊ Express gratitude
◊ Do yoga.
◊ Do qi gong or tai chi.
◊ Laugh
◊ Be creative.

Try doing some or all of these things and you'll see how much better you'll feel. Of course, it may not be easy to be "up" all the time, but you can certainly try!

In her book, "Frequency", Penney Peirce suggests that when you see others with low energy, "take the role of teacher or mentor and use your higher frequency for the greater good. Try setting the tone in a given situation because your personal vibration affects others as readily as theirs does you."

If you feel your energy dropping, bring yourself back to your "home frequency." To establish your home frequency, sit quiet and still and practice your yogic breathing. Now think about a time when you felt really, really great – the happiest you've ever been. Dive deep into the feeling and experience it completely. Picture the whole scene in as much detail as you can and be there, all over again, in your mind's eye. Stay with this feeling for a few minutes. This is your home frequency. Anytime you feel your energy dropping or others dragging it down, you can always bring yourself "home."

Peirce states, "When your frequency is high, you receive support, messages, opportunities and miracles and feel deserving and encouraged. You attract things that resonate with your vibrational level. You can think of it as energy waves being in synch with each other."

Oftentimes, you don't even realize that your energy is "in synch" with another person's until something happens to bring it to your attention. Sometimes you'll see or hear from someone whom you haven't seen or spoken to in a long time, but were recently thinking about. Sometimes just the right person will show up to help you just when you need them. And the most amazing thing, is that you may not even know the people who you're "in synch" with the most!

Please don't get lost in the concepts of energy and vibration. It's enough for you to know that we're all connected, we're all one and together we can all make positive changes for the planet.

Jason

Ever since Jason's parents were divorced, he traveled to Los Angeles to spend summer vacations with his Dad. Jason lived in a small town on the east coast and looked forward to the excitement of L.A. When Jason's Mom bought his plane ticket, he asked her to be sure to reserve a window seat for him. He wanted to become a pilot and liked to look out the window and imagine himself navigating the plane.

The day came for Jason to leave. He boarded the plane and found his seat. He pulled out his snacks from his backpack and put them in the pocket of the seat in front of him. He picked out the movies he wanted to watch, put on his headphones, covered himself with his blanket, took off his shoes and settled in for the long flight. As the plane filled up, he realized that he had lucked out. The seat next to him was empty. Now he could really get comfortable and stretch out a bit and he wouldn't have to make conversation with anyone, something he really didn't feel like doing.

After everyone was seated, just before takeoff, a middle-aged man asked the flight attendant if he could switch with someone who had a window seat. He was assigned a seat between two other people. He explained that he was extremely claustrophobic and there was no way that he could manage the long flight in that seat. The flight attendant approached Jason and asked him if he would be willing to switch seats. More than anything, Jason wanted to say no. The last place he wanted to sit was in between two other people plus he was already completely settled in. Jason looked over at the man and could see severe anxiety setting in. The man was visibly shaking, sweating and breathing fast. Jason felt badly for him. He realized that it wouldn't be such a big deal to move and help the man out. He gathered his things and exchanged seats. Not only was he now seated between two people who spoke to him non-stop, but his movie screen was broken. This was the worst trip he had ever taken.

The following week, Jason went shopping at the local pharmacy to get some things he needed for his stay. When he arrived, there were no more shopping carts or baskets available so he tried to carry everything he needed. Things kept falling out of his arms, so he shoved a few small things in his coat pockets. When he got to the cashier he placed everything on the counter, paid and approached the exit door. Suddenly he heard an alarm sound and the cashier yelled for him to stop. He couldn't figure out what was going on. The cashier called for the manager. While Jason waited for him, he realized that he had forgotten to empty his pockets of the things he had put in them. He tried to explain to the cashier that he had every intention of paying for them, but had forgotten they were there. The cashier didn't believe him so Jason started getting really scared. Would the manager believe him? Would his Dad believe him? What a way to start summer vacation! Suddenly, the manager appeared and Jason turned to speak to him. Immediately they both recognized each other. The manager was the man whom Jason had given his seat to on the plane! He knew that even though it was really inconvenient for Jason to switch seats with him, he did it because it was the right thing to do. He knew he couldn't be the type of kid that would shoplift. Jason paid for the items and headed home. He realized then how connected people are and how our lives intersect, even with people we don't even know.

To Say:
◊ I am connected to everything in the universe.
◊ I am connected to every other person on the planet.
◊ I choose to positively influence everyone around me.
◊ I choose to keep my energy high.

To Do:
Choose someone you know whom you haven't been in contact with for a long time. Pick one day to think about that person as often as you can throughout the day. If you like, you can imagine sending them positive energy. Then over the next day or two, see if they contact you. (This works most of the time, but if the person doesn't contact you, it may be that their energy is so low that they can't "pick-up" on your vibrations.)

Chapter 3

Tolerance And Acceptance

We are all one ... only egos, beliefs and fears separate us.

~ Unknown author

So, now that we've established that you matter and that everyone is connected, the next logical conclusion is that everyone matters, right? And if everyone matters then they belong here just as much as you do and they deserve to be treated the same way you expect to be treated.

So why are people so intolerant of each other? The above quote says it all. It may be because of ego. For some people to feel powerful they feel the need to make others feel weak. Or it may be because so many of us are raised with false beliefs and suspicions about other cultures and religions and are taught that if someone is different from us, then they're not as good as we are. The root of both ego and false beliefs is fear. Fear stemming from insecurity about oneself or fear of the unknown. When people act differently, talk differently or dress differently from you, it evokes fear because you may not understand it or you're not used to it.

So how do we get past the fear? By concentrating on our similarities and appreciating the differences and not being suspicious of them.

Everyone wants to be loved and respected. No one wants to be ridiculed or shunned. I have a friend who ends her emails with a quote "Be kinder than normal – everyone is fighting some kind of battle." This is so true. Every single person on this planet, no matter their race, religion, ethnicity or disability has at one time or another had the same emotions and feelings as every other person.

Try to approach everyone you meet from this perspective. Decide right now to try focusing on the "sameness" of those around you.

Remember that we all feel...

happiness

sadness

frustration

pain

anger

worry

anxiety

disappointment

joy

hope

And we all want to be....
loved
respected
appreciated
valued

There's a saying, "the eyes are the windows of the soul." You can tell so much about a person just by looking into their eyes. You'll see love, joy, sadness, and pain. All the same emotions that people see when they look back into your eyes.

When seeing or meeting someone different from you, rather than being judgmental, decide that what makes that person different may be something worth talking to them about and learning more about. Ignorance breeds fear. If you take the time to learn about other cultures and religions, you'll notice many similarities to your own and that will help make you more comfortable with the person. But, if there were too many similarities, life would be so boring, wouldn't it? Embrace the differences. It's so exciting to learn about other people's customs, food, dance, clothing, language, etc. This is what makes life interesting. That's how you grow.

Tyler

Tyler played soccer and he was good at it. His Dad and all his brothers had played and they expected him to join the school team when he was old enough. The problem was that Tyler didn't really like soccer, but he played because they wanted him to and it helped him be accepted by the "in crowd."

Tyler was afraid to say what he really wanted to do. He loved music and had dreamed of joining the band. This was completely unheard of in his family. "Only geeks join the band," his brothers would say. When no one knew, Tyler listened to classical music on his phone with his earphones so no one would know. He loved Bach and Beethoven. He would pretend that he was in a concert hall watching an orchestra play, and sometimes he imagined himself as the conductor. He couldn't tell any of his friends about his passion, especially the other guys on the team. They were all into hip hop and rock and wouldn't be able to relate.

Then Miguel showed up in Tyler's class, a new exchange student from Spain. He was a soccer star in his home town and the coach couldn't wait to get Miguel on the team. Tyler and Miguel played soccer together, but it was hard for Tyler to get used to Miguel. Tyler lived in a small American town and his family had never really traveled far. He had very little contact with people outside of his community.

It was difficult for Tyler to understand Miguel with his heavy Spanish accent. He didn't understand some of the customs he practiced or the way he interacted with the other players.

Tyler didn't really try to become friends with Miguel because he didn't think they had anything to talk about other than soccer and Tyler really didn't want to talk about that subject. Not only was Miguel from another country, he felt their lives were "worlds apart."

One day Miguel left his cellphone on the bench near the soccer field. Tyler picked it up to give it to him and noticed that he had been listening to a Beethoven symphony. He wasn't sure if Miguel also liked classical music or it just happened to show up on his phone by accident or maybe as part of an ad. Tyler was anxious to find out. Could it be that this guy who he thought he had absolutely nothing in common with also liked classical music? He wasn't sure how to find out without embarrassing himself.

A few days later, Tyler and some of the other players stopped by the house where Miguel was staying and picked him up for practice. Tyler volunteered to go in the house to get him. When he reached Miguel's room he heard his favorite

Beethoven symphony playing. He wasn't sure what to say about it so he just said, "interesting music." Miguel smiled and said, "I grew up listening to classical music. I love it. I listen to it a lot, especially when I'm feeling homesick."

Tyler was so happy that he finally found someone who shared his interest, someone else he could talk to about music. He never would have believed it would be someone who was so different from him in so many other ways. Later that day, Tyler did talk to Miguel about it and they ended up becoming really good friends. He realized then that every person does have something in common with every other person if we just take the time and make the effort to find out what it is.

To Say:
◊   Every person matters.
◊ · For every person I meet, I will look for our similarities and appreciate our differences.

To Do:
Pick someone in one of your classes or on your team whom you don't know very well.

Observe them for a few days. Be completely objective and non-judgmental.
◊   What kind of facial expressions do they make?

◊   How do they walk?
◊   How do they interact with other people?
◊   How do they talk?
◊   How do they dress?
◊   What are some things you notice that you have in common with this person?
◊   What is something different about the person that you want to learn more about?

Chapter 4

Opportunity

The golden opportunity you are seeking is in yourself. It is not in your environment; it is not in luck or chance, or the help of others; it is in yourself alone.

~ *Orison Swett Marden*

As I mentioned before, wonderful things happen when your energy is high. You attract new opportunities and miraculous things can happen. Miracles can and do happen everyday. But for miracles to happen, you must believe it's possible. If you go through life thinking that they can't happen to you, they most likely won't. But if you believe they can, they will. It's as simple as that.

You've heard the saying, "I'll believe it when I see it"? Wayne Dyer, the famous psychologist and author said, "If you believe it, you'll see it." Quite a difference, wouldn't you say?

This so accurately sums up conscious living. As I mentioned in the introduction to this book, conscious living is about opening up your mind and your heart and reaching past your limitations.

You must believe that ANYTHING is possible, because it is.

Opportunities are everywhere.

They are around every corner and can manifest themselves in strange and unexpected ways and at unexpected times. The key is to be receptive, believe that wonderful things can happen for you and to recognize an opportunity when it presents itself. Sometimes when opportunities do open up for you, it can be a bit scary and you may have trouble deciding if it's the right thing for you to do. Often it comes down to using your inner wisdom, your intuition, to guide you. I'll talk about this more in another chapter. The point I want to make now is that infinite possibilities exist at every moment of every day.

In her book, "The Law of Divine Compensation", Marianne Williamson writes, "How we think releases an infinite number of possibilities that could not have occurred had we not believed that they were possible."

Sometimes a perfect opportunity presents itself at exactly the right time, in exactly the right way and there's no question that it's the right thing for you to pursue. But sometimes an opportunity isn't completely apparent. It may not be just the right thing at the right time, but if you listen to your inner voice it will tell you that with just a little effort it will become the perfect path for you.

Many years ago, the doctor I was working with decided to close his practice, which left me looking for another position. One evening I attended a dinner lecture. I knew there would be several doctors there and I opened myself to infinite possibilities, hoping that I might get a lead on a new job. I entered the lecture room. It was open seating so I chose a table where a group of doctors were sitting. During the meal before the lecture, I made conversation with them, asked their names and where they practiced. They happened to all be from the same group. I introduced myself and asked them if they happened to be looking for a Physician Assistant. One of them told me they had just hired their first PA a few weeks before so they really weren't looking for another one so soon. I was so disappointed. They seemed like a nice group. The evening ended and I told them how much I enjoyed meeting them. As I drove home, I was still a bit disappointed, but something told me that I was led to that table for a reason and that I was meant to work for that group.

The next day I looked online for the name and address of one of the doctors and sent him a letter. I told him how much I enjoyed meeting him and his colleagues and wrote, "I know you just hired a PA, but if you decide to hire a second, I would very much like to be considered for the position." I mailed the letter and sent positive thoughts with it on its way.

Less than a week later, I received a letter back from the doctor. He wrote that they enjoyed meeting me as well. He said that they talked about me after the meeting and decided that since the PA they just hired had proved to be so valuable, they would hire another for one of their other offices. They asked if I would like to come in for an interview. I was so happy!

By following the lessons I was learning about conscious living I was able to recognize a potential opportunity, follow my intuition and think positively about the situation rather than let myself get discouraged. I interviewed for the job, was hired and worked for that group for 10 wonderful years.

Opening yourself up to unlimited possibilities may sometimes require you to take risks. When risk is involved, it may be because the opportunity isn't completely transparent, but that doesn't mean it's not the right opportunity. Sometimes, a bit of an obstacle might be put in your way so that you have to put in some effort to make the opportunity turn into a reality. This is part of growing and learning. The trick is to know when taking a risk has a good chance of you ending up on the right side of the situation. Again, this is when you step back, weigh all your options, get in tune with your inner wisdom and then jump into the opportunity if it feels right.

After working for the medical group for 10 years, I received a phone call from a researcher I knew from overseas. It was completely "out of the blue," totally unexpected. He offered me a position with a new company he was starting. It was exactly in my field of interest and sounded very exciting, but I would have to leave my job and move overseas. My husband and I thought about it, weighed all our options, the pros and the cons. I jumped into it headfirst and took the risk. It turned out to be one of the best decisions I ever made.

I want to be clear about something. The opportunities I'm talking about for you don't have to be big ones, like a new job, or moving to another country. Perhaps an exciting opportunity for you would be to be invited on a trip with a friend, to be given the chance to play in a new position on your sports team, to be invited to the dance by someone you have a crush on or to win a scholarship to the college of your dreams.

Just remember to be open and receptive, think positively, keep your energy high and believe that great things can and will happen to you. And they will.

Marcus

Marcus sat in science class on the first day of school and looked around the room at the other kids in his class. He recognized many of them from some of his classes the year before or had seen them in the hallways. As he scanned the room, his eyes landed on Tara. Tara was one of the most beautiful girls in school. Every guy in the 10th grade dreamed of dating her. Marcus was no exception. They had attended the same school since kindergarten, but they had never spoken. Marcus often thought about what it would be like to date Tara, but he really didn't know much about her. He did notice that she was kind and smart. He knew she would never be interested in someone like him. Marcus wasn't considered one of the popular guys in school. He didn't really know which "group" he belonged to. He was very tall and thin with a bad complexion. He tried to keep up with the latest clothing and hairstyles, even if he didn't like them, just so he wouldn't be made to feel like a complete "outsider." He liked to learn and read a lot. He loved history and archeology. So there he sat in his new science class, looking at Tara, thinking again about how cool it would be to get to know her.

Over the summer, Marcus started learning about conscious living. He read about how his thoughts create his reality and by how opening himself up to unlimited possibilities, they could really happen.

He decided that he would stop thinking of himself as someone who could never date someone like Tara and started thinking positively about himself. He had a lot of qualities that a girl would like if she only gave him a chance and got to know him. He starting saying his affirmations, "I matter", "I am an interesting person", "I am dating a nice, kind and beautiful girl." Little by little he gained more confidence and started to feel much better about himself.

The following week in science class, Ms. Grant announced to the class that they would be starting a two-week science project. It would be done in pairs. She gave half the class a set of numbers and the other half the same set of numbers. Everyone with the same numbers would be project partners. Of course, you guessed it, right? Marcus received the same number as Tara! He was nervous, knowing that they would be working closely together and he hoped that he wouldn't mess things up so he kept up his affirmations.

Over the two weeks of working together, the two got to know each other. It turned out that Tara was also interested in history so while doing their science experiment they would talk about interesting things they had read. Tara had seen Marcus around for years in school, but knew nothing about him. She was now given a chance to get to know who he really was. He had a great sense of humor and made her laugh and they had a lot of fun in class.

After the project was over, Marcus felt comfortable and confident enough to ask Tara to the Fall dance. He had really come to like her and felt that they had a real connection. She accepted his invitation and it was one of the happiest moments in his life.

As they danced, Marcus thought about how the night could be one of those "one-in-a-million" experiences or he could keep up his confidence and positive thinking and try to continue a relationship with Tara. Now that you're learning about conscious living, I'll let you create the end of the story!

To Say:
◊ Anything is possible.
◊ I am open to receiving new opportunities.
◊ Wonderful things can and will happen for me.

To Do:
Think of something you would really like to have happen to you. Think about what you can do

to help make it happen or what you may be doing that's keeping it from happening. Be honest with yourself.

Now, visualize the opportunity presenting itself to you. How would it make you feel? Try to experience the same emotions right now that you think you would have. Try to feel as though it has already happened. Think about this opportunity happening as often as you can and return to that same feeling each time. Just your thoughts and emotions can help you attract the right energy to help the opportunity become real.

Chapter 5

Open To Abundance

The world is full of abundance and opportunity, but far too many people come to the fountain of life with a sieve instead of a tank car ... a teaspoon instead of a steam shovel. They expect little and as a result they get little.

~ Ben Sweetland

Just like you can experience incredible opportunities by keeping your energy high, you can also attract other things into your life. You can attract joy, happiness, peace, love and even wealth. It's called abundance.

So many of us live from a place of lack – we feel that we never have enough and will never have enough. Many people believe they don't deserve abundance or that we were all put on this earth to suffer and struggle. Some believe that if they were to have everything they want and all is going well, something bad will eventually happen to take it all away. As the quote above says, if you think small, your life will have limits, if you think big, there is no limit to what you can have.

Similar to keeping your energy high, you can learn how to use your subconscious mind to bring wonderful things into your life.

In his book, "The Power of Your Subconscious Mind", Dr. Joseph Murphy teaches us how we can use our subconscious mind to create the reality of our dreams.

He states that "It was never intended that man should lead a life of indigence. You can have wealth, everything you need and plenty to spare."

Having wealth, however, shouldn't be your ultimate goal. It should only be the means to an end. What I mean is, once you learn how to shift your thinking and you start manifesting abundance, you have a responsibility to share it with others, to make a positive contribution to society and the planet.

Dr. Murphy explains that the first step in making this shift is to decide what you want and to be very clear about sending that information to your subconscious. The dominant idea is always accepted by the subconscious mind. You must think about being successful and having all that you need and want and avoid thinking negatively. He states that "wealth flows from you instead of to you."

He writes, "If you are full of fear about the future, you are also attracting negative conditions to you. Your subconscious mind takes your fear and negative statements as your request and proceeds in its own way to bring obstacles, delays, lack and limitation into your life." Also, if you are envious and jealous of what other people have, this is a sure-fire way to block the flow of prosperity to you. Try to be happy for other people when good things happen to them.

Once you learn to maintain thoughts of abundance and prosperity you will see amazing things happen in your life. Since your subconscious mind helps create your reality, it will take directions from you and create situations that will lead to wonderful things.

Sarah

Sarah had her eye on a red jacket she saw in the new store at the mall. She had wanted a red jacket for a long time, but the ones she had seen weren't the right shade of red, the right size or the style she wanted. She had been to the mall a week ago and went into the new store to check it out. There on a mannequin in the front window was the exact jacket she had been looking for. It was just the right shade of red, in the exact style and they had several in her size. The only problem was that she hadn't been able to find any work over the summer, so now that she found the perfect jacket, she didn't have the $30 to buy it and she didn't want to ask her parents for the money.

Sarah recently learned about opening herself up to receiving abundance, so she decided to focus on getting that jacket. She pictured herself trying it on in the store and it fit perfectly. She could imagine what the soft, red material would feel like and how it would keep her warm on windy, cold days. She pictured the saleswoman putting it in a bag and then Sarah would bring it home and hang it up in her closet. She imagined herself wearing it to school and to parties. She looked and felt amazing in it. She kept repeating in her mind "I have my red jacket and I love it!"

Soon after, Sarah's neighbor stopped by. She decided to go on a vacation, but the person who usually took care of her cat while she was away was out of town. She asked Sarah if she would mind taking care of Snowball for a few weeks. All she would have to do was feed her, play with her a bit and keep the litter box clean. Sarah liked her neighbor so she was more than happy to help. On the way out of Sarah's house, the neighbor turned back toward Sarah and said "Oh, by the way, I don't expect you to do this for nothing. I'll pay you $60 for your trouble." Sarah smiled and knew exactly what she was going to do with the money – she had enough to buy her jacket and one for her sister, too!

Okay, I know you're probably saying "this would never happen" or "it might happen to someone else, but not to me." This is where you're wrong. This does happen to people and it CAN happen to you. You have to learn to expect the unexpected.

I've had some major challenges in my life. For many years, whenever things were going well, I would always be waiting for the next bad thing to happen. I could never fully enjoy my life during times that should have been happy. When I learned about conscious living – that life can be great, that I could have everything I ever wanted, that bad things didn't have to happen, I shifted my thinking. I was tired of living the way I had been. And you know what? Miraculous changes happened in my life. Totally unexpected abundance manifested and I was "blown away."

A friend of mine used to say to me, "How come things always seem to go just right for you? The most amazing things just happen to come your way just at the right time." I shared the information with her that I'm sharing with you now. She could have made the change, but she didn't. You have the same choice. Make the change right now.

To Say:
◊   I have a right to be happy.
◊   I deserve to have success.
◊   I am open to abundance.
◊   I accept prosperity into my life.

To Do:
◊   Think of something you want to have.
    Say out loud to yourself, "I want to have
    _____."
◊   What does the thing look like?
◊   What size is it?
◊   What color is it?
◊   What does it feel like?
◊   How do you feel when you're holding or
    touching it?
◊   What do you look like when you're feeling
    or touching it?

Get a very clear picture of the entire scene and then replay this in your mind every night before you go to bed and every morning when you wake up.

Chapter 6

Knowledge Is Power

The pursuit of knowledge is never-ending. The day you stop seeking knowledge is the day you stop growing.

~ *Brandon Travis Ciaccio*

Now that you know HOW to attract abundance into your life, you need to figure out WHAT you want to attract. To know what you want you must be willing to learn about the treasures that lie beyond your limited existence. There's a whole world of fascinating people, places and things just waiting for you to experience.

When I was growing up, we didn't have the Internet. I remember a set of encyclopedias on a shelf in our living room. Each book had subjects listed alphabetically. One book was A through C, one book was D through F and so on. I remember how exciting it was when my parents bought the set. We would sit for hours on the living room floor combing through the books reading about different subjects and looking at the pictures. The one that interested me the most was the section on the human body. It had clear flaps, each printed with a different body system and you would lay the flaps over each other one at a time to reveal the entire body. It was fascinating to me and I would return to that section often, looking at the pictures of all the organs, blood vessels and nerves. As I got older, I began reading the description of the flaps and learning about how the body works. Who knows, this may be what planted the seed that eventually led me to practice medicine.

Now with the Internet, you have the entire world laid out in front of you. You can learn about anything, at any time, with just the touch of a finger.

Be curious!

Once you start learning about things outside the limits of your life, you can decide what you want to attract to help enrich your life and help you become your best self.

Maybe you'd like the chance to visit the Geopark in Braunwald, Switzerland or the oldest freestanding stone buildings on the island of Malta.

Like music? How about attending a seven-day music festival in Roskilde, Denmark or the music festival, Fuji Rock, in Japan?

Maybe you'd like a chance to learn aikido, a type of martial art or find out how to make the

Indian dish, malai kofta.

How would you know that you might want to become a forensic psychologist if you don't even know what they do?

Find joy in learning new things. Never be satisfied with what you know now. Always strive to broaden your horizons, then share your knowledge with others.

Caitlin

Ever since Caitlin was a little girl, she was interested in fashion. She would play dress-up every chance she got. Her mom would buy clothing at second-hand stores so Caitlin would always have plenty of clothes to play with. She would add her mother's jewelry and scarves to make each outfit as nice as she could. When Caitlin learned to draw, she would make pictures of girls with pretty dresses, shirts and pants. She dreamed of becoming a fashion designer one day.

Caitlin was now in high school and she still had the same goal. She continued to create drawings of different fashions, but was becoming bored with the same basic designs with just a few additions here and there. Since she was serious about her career aspirations, she decided she would start learning more about fashion. She got on the Internet and learned about the most famous designers. She learned about their backgrounds and the inspirations for their designs. She studied about different kinds of traditional dress from around the world – the sari from India, kilts from Scotland, dirndls from Austria, flamenco dresses from Spain, kimonos from Japan and many others. She practiced drawing these over and over and became quite good at it.

One day as Caitlin was exploring the Internet she came across an international contest for high school students interested in fashion design. They were asking for an original design and the best one would be awarded a prize. Caitlin decided right then that she wasn't going to miss this golden opportunity. She had been studying fashion a lot lately and was confident that she could come up with a unique and beautiful creation. She said her affirmations about attracting abundance and told herself that she was capable of winning.

Caitlin worked very hard on her design in her spare time. She used all the knowledge she had learned about traditional dress from around the world and took bits and pieces of each one. She thought about some of the ideas that some of the great designers had had over the years and why they picked those particular designs to make. Soon Caitlin finished her creation and it was magnificent. There was a lot of detail and she used the most beautiful colors. It was truly a work of art. She submitted her entry and waited anxiously for the contest to announce the winner.

A few weeks later, Caitlin received an email. The organizers of the contest wrote to her that her entry was the best by far. She showed true imagination and creativity and they could tell that she had learned a lot about fashion design. They could tell that she had spent a lot of time on her project and was serious about it.

Caitlin won first prize. She was ecstatic! She was given free tuition and airfare to a summer internship at the Ecole de la Chambre Syndicale, school of fashion design in Paris, France. Caitlin was so happy then that all her fact-finding and exploring had paid off and she was headed straight toward her lifelong goal.

To Say
◊   To be my best self, I will learn as much as I can.
◊   I enjoy learning new things.
◊   Knowledge is the gateway to all good things.

To Do
Every week, pick a topic to explore and learn about. Take notes and write down questions you may have about the topic, then explore some more. Topics can include places, famous people,

foods, technology, careers, music, art, medicine, religion, history, politics, etc. First pick topics that you have a special interest in, but then branch out and learn about things that you know nothing about or have no interest in (or so you thought!).

Chapter 7

Be Present

"Forget yesterday – it has already forgotten you. Don't sweat tomorrow – you haven't even met. Instead, open your eyes and your heart to a truly precious gift – today."

~*Steve Maraboli*

Now that you know how to train your subconscious to manifest abundance, and know what you want to manifest, you must learn how to focus your mind – make it laser sharp so it will work for you to help you be your best self. The most effective way to do this is by staying present or what some call practicing mindfulness. All this means is concentrating on the present moment – paying close attention to what you're currently experiencing, no matter what you're doing or where you are. Being mindful is about noticing the details of what you see around you, what you smell, what you feel, and the sounds you hear.

It's called staying present because you block out thoughts of the past and the future. You only concentrate on what's going on at this moment.

We have thousands of thoughts every day, most of them are pretty negative. We think about things we did or things that happened to us in the past and instead of learning from our mistakes and redirecting ourselves we tend to dwell on the negative and become depressed or feel regret. Unfortunately, we typically don't think about the good times we've had.

When we think about the future, instead of setting goals or dreaming about a wonderful life ahead we usually focus on "what ifs" and become fearful and anxious. We make up entire stories about what will or could happen, most of which never occur. We waste our whole lives living in times that don't exist – the past and future. All that is ever real is this present moment.

We also tend to avoid the present moment by losing ourselves in our cellphones, TV, movies or video games. All of these technologies are useful and have a place in our lives, but we have to be careful not to forget about the real world, this moment and all that it has to offer.

Think about how much goes through your mind every day, every hour, every minute. If you had someone hanging out with you that talked to you as much as you talk to yourself, you would probably try to stay away from them as much as you could. It's what some call the "wild elephant" or the "monkey mind."

It takes practice to quiet your mind and stay present, but you can train yourself to do it. When you stay present, your mind conserves energy and then is always ready to recognize and act when opportunities come your way.

In "How to Train a Wild Elephant", Dr. Jan Chozen Bays defines mindfulness as "deliberately paying full attention to what is happening around you and within you – in your body, heart and mind. Mindfulness is awareness without criticism or judgment."

Think about a time when you were in the middle of an emergency or a similar situation where you were abruptly drawn away from your thoughts and directly into the present moment. You paid attention to what was going on at that precise moment with no regard to the past or future. Being in the moment can be exhilarating. That's why so many people love doing extreme sports and other potentially dangerous activities because it forces them to be intensely in the moment. If they were to stray from that moment, it could mean injury or even death.

Dr. Chozen Bays explains that much research has been done on mindfulness and studies show that those who try to practice it regularly "are models of flourishing and positive mental health."

Try it right now. Look around you. What do you see? Look closely, like you were looking at it for the first time. What do you smell? What sounds do you hear? Feel your clothes touching you or your weight against the place that you're sitting. When you live in the present moment, life becomes richer. Colors seem more vibrant, you'll notice things you never noticed before. You don't just hear sounds, but you listen with a different ear. You feel more alive and you appreciate the world around you so much more.

Nick

Nick pulled out his suitcase from the closet and started packing for sailing camp in South Carolina. He had always wanted to go, but it was expensive so he didn't want to ask his parents to send him, especially since he had four brothers and sisters.

Recently, someone donated money to his school so students could attend summer programs. He applied for a scholarship and was accepted.

His dream had come true! The only problem was that he still wasn't happy. Nick's dad had been laid off from work and he was having trouble finding a new job. He was putting pressure on Nick's mom to look for work. His mom had always stayed at home and she was very anxious about going out into the work world. Because of the financial pressures, his parents had been arguing a lot lately. He was happy to be able to escape for the summer, but worried about what would happen while he was gone. He was the oldest child and felt that it was his responsibility to keep the family together.

Nick arrived at camp in South Carolina. It was absolutely beautiful, but he hardly noticed the scenery. He couldn't stop thinking about his parents. Other campers tried to make friends with him, but he didn't really feel like making conversation. He learned about sailing and enjoyed being on the boat, but kept wondering what was going on at home. He was thinking about so many "what if" possibilities that it affected his summer experience.

◊   Maybe he shouldn't have gone to camp.
◊   Maybe he should have looked for a summer job instead so he could help out.
◊   Maybe his mom wouldn't be able to find work and they wouldn't be able to pay their bills, or they would become homeless.
◊   Maybe things would get so bad, his parents would get divorced.
◊   What would he do then?
◊   Who would he live with?
◊   Who would his brothers and sisters live with?

His mind kept racing day after day. One day while on the boat, he was sitting and thinking and all of a sudden, he felt like he had been hit with a hard fist. Because he hadn't been paying attention, the sail had quickly spun around in the other direction and hit him square on the right side of his head. He became lightheaded and a bit disoriented. After he got himself together, he fixed the sail. He looked out over the water and realized that he had better stay present, at least while he was on the boat, so he wouldn't make the same mistake.

At the end of the summer, Nick packed his things to return home. He hadn't spoken to his parents for over a week. He called his mom to let her know when to expect him. His mom was so happy to hear from him.

"Nick," she said, "you won't believe it! Your dad found a job! It's a position he's always wanted and he's going to be making even more money than he was before. We're so relieved. We can't wait to see you. Did you have fun?"

At that point, Nick was happy for his family, but he realized that he had wasted the entire summer thinking about what might have happened. He completely missed out on enjoying the scenery, making friends and having, what could have been, the best summer of his life. He learned a valuable lesson about mindfulness that day.

To Say

◊   The present moment is all I ever have.

◊   I will make each moment count.

◊   I will use all my senses to appreciate the world around me.

To Do

◊   Look at a tree. Notice its height, the way the limbs branch out and the way the roots align themselves, if you can see them.

◊   Look at the leaves. What color are they? What shape are they? Notice the veins running through them, carrying nourishment to every part.

◊   Look at the bark. What color is it? Is it rough or smooth? Are there insects living there?

◊   Does the tree have a smell? What do the leaves and the bark feel like?

◊   Listen to the sounds the leaves make as the wind blows around them.

Chapter 8

Dare To Be Creative

To live a creative life, we must lose our fear of being wrong.

~ *Joseph Chilton Pearce*

When you learn to live in the present moment, not only does your mind become sharper, but you become more creative as well. Because you're not living in the past or future, your mind is able to focus and become connected to your imagination in a fun and positive way.

Being creative isn't just about being talented, like being a great artist, musician, dancer or writer. Creativity is in all of us. We can all be creative in some way. Studies have shown that we're all very creative as young children, but we lose that part of us as we age. Our creativity gets stifled because most of us are afraid of what others may think when we share our creations. Of course, this attitude only creates anxiety and fear, which puts the brakes on creativity altogether.

Maybe you do have a special talent, but you haven't been given the right environment to discover it. Maybe you would be really good at some type of art form you've never even heard of or an instrument from another country that you've never even seen. Maybe you just haven't been inspired enough.

If you like to draw, you don't need a fancy set of pastels or charcoals and an artist pad. Pick up a pencil, a pen, a crayon and a piece of notebook paper or even a napkin! Just start and then let yourself go. Reach deep inside and let your thoughts and feelings flow out of your hands.

If you like to sing, sing. You don't need to be good enough for the X Factor to express yourself through song.

If you want to dance, dance. Dance in the privacy of your room, if you want. Just do it! The key is to have fun and express your inner feelings in whichever way calls to you.

If you want to write, then write. Write a short story, a poem, a song. Just write. Just use your imagination and let go. You know, I have never written a book before. The idea for this book just came to me, so I sat down and started writing.

If you don't feel comfortable doing any of these things, remember that you can also express your creativity while doing daily tasks and discover the joy of creativity in everyday life.

◊   Redecorate your bedroom

◊ Use some new cosmetics
◊ Plan a party
◊ Put a new outfit together,
◊ Set a holiday table for your family.

Ethan

Ethan headed over to his neighbor's house. He had agreed to babysit their eight-year-old son for the weekend. Mr. and Mrs. Patton both had to attend weekend seminars for their jobs and needed someone to stay with Lucas. Ethan agreed to do it because he needed the money and he didn't have any plans. One of his friends was a good guitar player and was practicing with his band all weekend. His other buddy was into hip hop and had entered a dance contest so he was also busy practicing. Ethan didn't have any special talents or hobbies. He mainly watched TV and played video games so when he was asked to babysit, he said okay since he could do that just as well at the Pattons as he could do it at home. Plus he would be making money doing it, and Lucas was a good kid so it wouldn't be hard to watch him.

Ethan walked in the door and said hi to the Pattons. They gathered up their suitcases, kissed Lucas good-bye and headed out to their car. Ethan turned to Lucas and asked him what he wanted to do. He said that he had a friend coming over soon to play. When Lucas' friend arrived, they went outside in the yard, so Ethan straightened up the living room a bit and then went down to the guest room in the basement to unpack. The guest room was in the far corner and as he made his way to it, he noticed a big wooden table with a plastic cover over it. Of course, he was curious about what was underneath so he took a peak. As he lifted the cloth he saw small train tracks, model trains and a few little plastic trees strewn around. Everything was covered with a thick layer of dirt and dust. Later when Lucas came in, Ethan asked him about the train set. He told him that his half-brothers played with it when they were younger, but they were away at college and so it just sat there. Lucas knew it was there, but he had no interest in it.

That night, after he put Lucas to bed, Ethan sat down to watch TV, but he couldn't find anything that he wanted to watch. He decided to go down to his room and read a book. On his way to his room, he stopped again at the table. He lifted up the cloth and started picking up pieces of the train set to look at them more closely. He noticed the small, intricate details of each train car and the little faces of the toy people. He took everything off, dusted off the wooden table and then cleaned off each piece. He connected the train tracks together, but there weren't enough to make a complete circle. He looked around and against the wall, saw several boxes filled with more track, bridges, more people, trees and all kinds of other accessories. He didn't think the Pattons would mind if he took out some of the pieces.

After he pulled out each piece and cleaned it off, he turned to the table and carefully set it down in its place. Ethan became entranced. He spent all night designing the track so that it wound its way around the small town he had set up, running it over small plastic mountains and under bridges. He set up trees alongside the tracks and turned the small houses and shops into a tiny little town. He had people set up in the park, outside stores and he used others as railroad workers. Never in his wildest dreams would Ethan have thought that he would be interested in something like a model train set. But he was having so much fun and he was enjoying doing something creative.

The next morning when Lucas woke up, Ethan showed him what he had made that night. Lucas' eyes lit up! He hadn't been interested in it because it was in the basement and it was dirty so he never wanted to go near the table.

Ethan and Lucas played with the trains for hours, watching them go around the town and imagining all kinds of scenarios. Ethan was almost disappointed when the Pattons returned home. They were so pleased to see what Ethan had accomplished and how much fun Lucas was having. They told Ethan he could come over any time to work on his new project, but he decided to set up his own table at home. He started collecting different parts and soon had an incredible set-up and had so much fun!

To Say:
◊ I am creative.
◊ I can imagine anything I want and turn it into reality.
◊ I am inspired.

To Do:
◊ Look around your bedroom. Is it time for a change?
◊ Would you like to do some redecorating? You can be creative by hanging some new pictures or posters.
◊ You can buy some small piece of furniture at a second-hand store and paint it any color you want.
◊ You can change the curtains just by hanging up some sheets with a pretty pattern on them or with the logo of your favorite sports team.
◊ You can put down a small rug that you like.

Let your mind go free and express yourself in your private space so that you feel inspired whenever you enter it.

Chapter 9

Lovingkindness

Perhaps everything terrible is, in its deepest being, something that needs our love.

~ Rainer Maria Rilke

Because you matter, you expect and deserve love and kindness from others. Because everyone else matters, they also deserve the same from you. By treating others with lovingkindness you positively affect them, but you also reap benefits from the act just as much or maybe even more. Giving of yourself raises your energy to very high levels and attracts wonderful things into your life. Of course, we should all be kind to one another without expecting something in return, but if everyone can benefit from an act of kindness, this makes it even more special.

Lovingkindness is much more than love or kindness. It's showing compassion and empathy for those in need. It's showing respect to others. It's accepting an apology from someone and offering forgiveness. It's avoiding an argument by trying to see the situation from the other person's perspective. It's doing volunteer work. It's protecting the kid in school who gets bullied. It's picking something up from the store for a neighbor who can't get out. Every one of us has unlimited opportunities for practicing lovingkindness every single day.

Maria

Almost every day, for the last several years, when Maria came home from school, Mr. and Mrs. Gonzalez would be sitting in rocking chairs on their balcony. She didn't know them very well. They were a quiet, elderly couple and kept to themselves. They didn't really socialize with anyone else in the neighborhood. Because of this, Maria often heard rumors that they were mean and unfriendly and it was best to ignore them.

Sometimes as she entered the front door of her apartment building, Maria would look their way and Mrs. Gonzalez would look back and nod her head, but she never spoke. It was like the two of them were permanent fixtures, the same as the light post, the stairs and the sidewalk.

If Maria was having a bad day, she would look up at them rocking back and forth and would be comforted by the familiarity of the situation and knew that tomorrow was another day. Hopefully it would be better. Of course, there were no guarantees, but at least she could count on Mr. and Mrs. Gonzalez being on their balcony at 5 p.m. and in some strange way that comforted her.

One day, Maria came home from a friend's house and when she hopped onto the first step of her building, she glanced up at the Gonzalez's balcony. She was surprised to see only Mr. Gonzalez in his rocking chair. The other chair was empty. Maria figured that his wife was in the apartment, probably fixing something to eat.

For the next few days, Maria noticed, again, Mr. Gonzalez rocking back and forth in his white rocking chair alone. No Mrs. Gonzalez. The season had changed and it was blistering hot out. Perhaps it was too hot for Mrs. Gonzalez to sit outside. After several more days of seeing the empty rocking chair, Maria decided to call up to Mr. Gonzalez and ask him where his wife was.

"Mr. Gonzalez, I see that you've been sitting outside by yourself. Where's your wife?"

"She passed," he replied as he turned his head away from Maria to hide his tears.

"Do you mind if I come up to speak to you for a minute?" asked Maria.

"That'll be fine," said Mr. Gonzalez, "the door's unlocked."

Maria spent the next two hours rocking next to Mr. Gonzalez. She asked him about his wife and found out the reason they rarely communicated with anyone was because Mr. Gonzalez was blind and Mrs. Gonzalez was deaf. They had had a very hard life with a lot of tragedy and heartbreak and no other family. They had been together for 68 years and had been deeply in love. Mr. Gonzalez's heart was broken and he felt so alone.

Maria knew then that there was only one thing for her to do. A few evenings a week she made a point of visiting Mr. Gonzalez and sit in the empty rocking chair. She would tell him about her day and her problems and Mr. Gonzalez would give her advice and share the wisdom he had gained from a long life of experience.

Maria grew to treasure this time with him and no longer saw Mr. Gonzalez as just a "permanent fixture." He became an important part of her life and a true friend.

To Say:
◊　I choose to do good.
◊　I choose to be kind.

To Do:
Think of different ways you can show kindness to those around you.
◊　Stand up for someone being bullied
◊　Buy dessert for the person standing next to you in line in the cafeteria
◊　Thank a teacher
◊　Do a chore at home without being asked
◊　Do something nice for an elderly couple in your neighborhood.

The opportunities are endless.

Chapter 10

Inner Knowing

Intuition is seeing with your soul.
~ *Dean Koontz*

We all have the innate gift of intuition. It's that little voice you hear or the feeling you get in the pit of your stomach that says either "Don't you dare do this" or "This may be the best thing that ever happened to you."

When people say "My mind tells me one thing, but my heart says another", intuition is neither of these. It's not thinking or feeling. It's an actual "knowing." Your intuition usually speaks to you in an instant. It's a powerful tool that is always available to you. You just need to be open to it, listen and pay attention. Sylvia Clare, in her book "Trust Your Intuition", describes it in these ways:

◊   A sudden flash of insight
◊   A predictive dream
◊   A spinal shiver of recognition as something is occurring or being told to you
◊   A sense of knowing something already
◊   A sense of déjà vu
◊   A snapshot image of a future scene or event

Take these signs seriously, especially if you have a bad feeling about something. It's your body's way of communicating with you to keep you safe and protected. How many times have you gone against your intuition only to have regrets about it later? How many times have you been in the middle of saying or doing something that you know you shouldn't be saying or doing, but you do it anyway? You rationalize, believing that your mind knows best. It's not easy, but if you pay attention, you can fine-tune your intuition so it becomes stronger and with practice you will learn to follow it more and more.

Dylan

It was the end of the school year and all of Dylan's friends were having graduation parties to celebrate the culmination of four long years of demanding teachers, piles of homework and never-ending exams. Dylan was well-liked so he was invited to all of them. He loved having the chance to hang out with his friends before everyone went their separate ways.

One afternoon, Dylan received a text message that Joe was having a pool party on Saturday. When he first read the message something inside told him that he shouldn't go, but he dismissed the feeling. He was happy to have one more chance to see everyone plus a girl he liked would probably be going, too.

On the morning of the party the feeling came back, the one that told him not to go. Dylan couldn't shake the feeling so he started to take it seriously. He had been working on shifting his thinking and getting more in touch with his intuition. When it came time to leave for the party, Dylan decided not to go. It was a hard decision, but he had started to learn to trust his feelings.

Later that night while Dylan was watching TV his phone buzzed. It was a text message from one of his buddies about the party. His friend had written that things had been going well and everyone was having fun, but the noise got a little out of hand and one of the neighbors called the police. Little did anyone know, but some guy that no one knew crashed the party. He had gone outside to get high, just about the time the cops showed up. Because they smelled the pot, they closed down the party and made everyone go down to the police station for questioning. It all worked out okay for Dylan's friends in the end, but Dylan was so glad that he listened to his intuition and spared himself an experience that could have ended badly for everyone.

To Say:
◊ I have innate wisdom that can help guide me.

◊   I trust my intuition.
◊   I will follow my intuition.

To Do:

For three nights in a row, before going to sleep, lie still and do the following:

◊   Think about a happy experience. Concentrate on how you feel while picturing the scene. Concentrate on the feeling in the middle of your chest and upper abdominal area.
◊   Next, do the opposite. Think about a time when you were angry or sad. Again, concentrate on how you feel while recalling this experience as you did before.

On the fourth night, think about something that you need to make a decision about.

◊   Say the first choice out loud. Notice the feeling in your chest and abdomen without thinking about it.
◊   Now state the second choice and do the same thing.

Note which of the two choices gives you an immediate positive feeling. This is usually the right choice for you.

If it doesn't work the first time, keep practicing. You have this gift and it will work eventually. Once you are in touch with it, it will never leave you.

Chapter 11

Be The Gatekeeper

It is our choices that show what we truly are, far more than our abilities.

~ J.K. Rowling

Scientists have recently discovered that the thin membrane that surrounds every cell in our bodies is one of the most important parts of the cell. It's made up of molecules that align themselves in such a way that there is strict control over what is allowed in and what can leave. Only those things that will benefit the cell can enter and only those things that should leave the cell can leave it. This goes on in every single one of the trillions of cells in your body every moment of every day.

You are like one giant cell. You face choices every single day about what you should allow into your body and mind and what leaves by way of your mouth and your body language.

You're exposed to tons of different messages, facts and ideas every day. You have complete control over what you internalize and allow to form your belief system. You also have control over what you put in your body. Is it for your ultimate good? How will it affect you later, in the long term? Will it help your body function at its optimum so that you can accomplish your goals? Will it feel good now, but have bad effects later. You are no longer a little kid. You now know the consequences of your actions and can make intelligent choices. The choices you make now will affect you for years to come.

Just like you have a choice as to what enters your body and mind, you have control over what leaves. The gateway to the outside is your mouth and your body language. You have complete control over both. Words are forever. Once you say something, those words can never be taken back. THINK before you speak.

Remember that just like there are consequences to what you allow in, there are consequences for what you allow out as well.

Paulette

Paulette's dad had recently been transferred by his employer to another city and it was Paulette's first day at her new high school. She was in a bit of a shock. Her last high school was very small. Everyone had been together since grade school and she knew everyone very well. Paulette had a lot of friends. Some were good students, like her, and some were not so good. Some were into sports, like her, and some weren't. Some were in the band, some were in art club, some were in drama club and some liked student government. She had always enjoyed having such a broad range of friends. Now she had to figure out where she fit in at this huge school. She had heard horror stories about big schools where there were tons of different cliques and kids were judgmental and there were even gangs.

After a few days, Paulette started making friends. It wasn't hard for her. She was very pretty with long, thick, curly brown hair and bright green eyes. She always kept up with the current style of clothes, always looked great, was friendly and had a good sense of humor. A group of girls started asking Paulette to sit with them in the school cafeteria at lunchtime. They were also very pretty girls and were considered some of the most popular in school. She was so happy that she was finally fitting in.

Every day for the next few weeks, Paulette sat with her new friends. At first they would talk about how they did on tests that day or how much homework they had. But the conversation always turned to gossip – who was dating who, who had gotten into trouble, who's parents were getting divorced, what teacher got angry that day. Then things got worse. They started trashing people – who was ugly, who was weird, who was gay, who dressed funny.

At first, Paulette felt uncomfortable. Her friends never talked like that at her old school. She was friends with everyone. But here she wanted to fit in and soon found herself acting and speaking just like her new friends.

One day, she sat down to eat lunch and one of the girls was laughing and talking about a boy she had seen in the schoolyard earlier that day. She said he was in a lower grade and she saw him "walking funny." She stood up and imitated the boy's walk and the other girls started laughing.

All of a sudden Paulette realized something. Could it be her younger brother they were talking about? He had been in a car accident a few years ago and since then he couldn't walk right. Paulette asked the girl to describe what the boy looked like and the clothes he had on. Sure enough, it was Tim, her brother.

Suddenly, Paulette felt a pain in her stomach. She realized not only how these girls were acting, but how she had let herself become just like them. She decided right then that she no longer wanted to be part of this group and distanced herself from them beginning the very next day. It took her a little while, but eventually she found her place with a new group of friends who were much kinder and more understanding.

To Say:
◊   I am the gatekeeper. I choose what I let into my mind and body and what I allow out.
◊   I choose those things that help me be my best self.

To Do:
Make a list of things that you face every day that you have a choice about. It could be what you eat, the movies and TV shows you watch, the music you listen to, the people you hang out with or what you say. Go through your list and decide which of these things you could improve upon to help keep your energy high and help make you feel good about yourself.

Chapter 12

Gratitude

Be thankful for what you have; you'll end up having more. If you concentrate on what you don't have, you will never, ever have enough.

~ Oprah Winfrey

This is the last chapter, Gratitude, because to me, it is the most important. I wanted to leave you with gratitude being foremost in your mind. It is the main path to being your best self, the one from which all the other paths of conscious living get their power from. Be thankful for everything you have and know that soon you will have even more to be grateful for.

When I started counting my blessings, my whole life turned around.

~ Willie Nelson

Say "thank you" often. Say it to your parents, your friends, your teachers, your coaches, your neighbors, the cashier in the grocery store, the maintenance man at your school, your bus driver. Let those two words be the last two words you say before you fall asleep at night and the first two words you say when you wake up. You will be amazed how just those two small words will completely transform your life.

With every thank you, you share a part of yourself with another person. They experience an opening of your heart, an exchange of positive and uplifting energy. It shows them that you are a person of worth and it makes them feel special.

It is impossible to feel grateful and depressed in the same moment.

~ *Naomi Williams*

For this chapter, I want you to be the main character in the story. I want you to write about something you're grateful for. It doesn't have to be something big. It can be a simple thing.

◊   Maybe you witnessed a beautiful sunset last night.
◊   Maybe you found something you lost.
◊   Maybe you finished an assignment on time that you never thought you would complete.
◊   Maybe all your friends got the flu, but you didn't.
◊   Maybe you got the exact present for your birthday that you were hoping for.
◊   Maybe you received a much better grade on a test than you thought you would.

There are a million things to be thankful for. Find one and be thankful for it with all your heart.

Gratitude is the foundation upon which you create your best self.

To Say:
◊   Thank you.
◊   I am grateful for all that I have.

To Do:
Every night before falling asleep, think of three things that happened that day that you're grateful for. It can be something seemingly insignificant or something great. It can even be that you're grateful that a certain thing DIDN'T happen. Doing this will shift your mindset and help you attract even more things to be grateful for. You'll fall asleep with a change of attitude that can lead to more restful sleep and a brighter tomorrow.

Watch this TED talk (stick with it through the introduction. You'll be glad you did):
https://www.ted.com/talks/
louie_schwartzberg_nature_beauty_gratitude

Postscript

I hope that you have enjoyed reading this book as much as I enjoyed writing it. My hope is for you to allow these ideas to enter your mind and heart and use them to make the best life possible for yourself and for those around you. If we all did this, just think how we could change the world and the future of our planet.

I want to hear from you. Please contact me at guidetoconsciousliving@gmail.com and follow me on Facebook at https://www.facebook.com/guidetoconsciousliving/?ref=bookmarks.

*Scan the QR code
to connect with Kathy Poodiack*

Recommended Reading

The Field, by Lynne McTaggart

Frequency, by Penney Peirce

The Law of Divine Compensation, by Marianne Williamson

The Power of Your Subconscious Mind, by Dr. Joseph Murphy

How to Train a Wild Elephant, by Jan Chozen Bays, MD

Trust Your Intuition, by Sylvia Clare

Your 3 Best Super Powers, Meditation, Imagination and Intuition, by Sonia Choquette

The Chemistry of Connection, by Patrick Holford

Big Magic, Creative Living Beyond Fear, by Elizabeth Gilbert

The Courage to be Creative, by Doreen Virtue

Don't Let Anything Dull Your Sparkle, By Doreen Virtue

Consciousness, The New Currency, by Brandon Bays and Kevin Billett

The Power of Now, by Eckhart Tolle

Embracing the Now, by Gina Lake

10 Secrets for Success and Inner Peace, by Dr. Wayne Dyer

Being in Balance, by Dr. Wayne Dyer

Living an Inspired Life, by Dr. Wayne Dyer

Becoming Aware, by Lisa Garr

Feel Free to Prosper, by Marilyn Jenett

E^2, by Pam Grout

E^3, by Pam Grout

Thank and Grow Rich, by Pam Grout

The Biology of Belief, by Dr. Bruce Lipton

The Intuitive Way by Penney Peirce

Made in the USA
Coppell, TX
29 November 2020

42374674R10059